Saint Joseph
ALTARS

Saint Joseph
ALTARS

Photography and Text by
Kerri McCaffety

PELICAN PUBLISHING COMPANY
Gretna 2003

The word "Pelican" and the depiction of a pelican are trademarks of Pelican Publishing Company, Inc., and are registered in the U.S. Patent and Trademark Office.

Library of Congress Cataloging-in-Publication Data

McCaffety, Kerri.
    Saint Joseph altars : photography and text / by Kerri McCaffety.
        p. cm.
    Includes bibliographical references (p.   ) and index.
    ISBN 1-58980-140-7
    1. Joseph, Saint—Cult—Louisiana—New Orleans. 2. Altars—Louisiana—New Orleans. 3. New Orleans (La.)—Religious life and customs. 4. Italian Americans—Louisiana—New Orleans—Religion. 5. Joseph, Saint—Cult—Louisiana—New Orleans—Pictorial works. 6. Altars—Louisiana—New Orleans—Pictorial works. 7. New Orleans (La.)—Religious life and customs—Pictorial works. 8. Italian Americans—Louisiana—New Orleans—Religion—Pictorial works. I. Title
    BT690 .M33 2003
    247'.1—dc21
                        2003010484

Front jacket: *Saint Joseph Church, Gretna*
Back jacket: *Anise cookies*
Page 2: *Fausto's Kitchen in Metairie*
Page 4: Top: *Tony Marino's altar in the French Quarter* Middle: *Anise cookies* Bottom: *Cake at the Center of Jesus the Lord*
Pages 6-7: *Tony Marino's altar in the French Quarter*
Page 11: *Detail from the altar of Marie and Caryl Fagot*
All photographs by Kerri McCaffety, except those on pages 17, 26 left, 40, 50, and 104 (by Katherine Slingluff) and pages 24 and 25 (by Syndey Byrd).

Printed in Singapore

Published by Pelican Publishing Company, Inc.
1000 Burmaster Street, Gretna, Louisiana 70053

CONTENTS

Acknowledgments

For generosity and recipes, I owe gratitude to Gene Bourg, John Mariani, Allain Bush, Poppy Tooker, Patty Marino, Irene DiPietro, Emeril, Roy Liuzza, and Pauline Canalito.

I am indebted to many scholars and journalists who did great research and writing on the subject, especially David C. Estes, Ph.D., Nancy Piatkowski, and Ethelyn Orso, and to the St. Joseph Guild for their wonderful booklet, *Viva San Giuseppe: A Guide to Saint Joseph Altars*. (Nearly everyone who gives an altar has a well-worn copy.)

Thanks to two fabulous photographers, Kat Slingluff, for frantically shooting with me (twenty altars in two days), and Syndey Byrd, for her important images.

Thanks to everyone at Pelican Publishing for the opportunity to do this project.

But mostly, thank you to the people whose hard work keeps this tradition alive. The gracious folks who welcomed me to their altars, told me their stories, and tried to feed me made this documentary possible, especially Tony Marino, Frances Benetrix, and Lillian Moran.

Thank you to Marie and Caryl Fagot, Glenda and Mike Lubrano, Angel Chevolleau and Candy Schlumbrecht, the Rau Family (especially Betty), Madeline Bernard and Camille Meranta, Robert Zanca, Miriam Murphy, Buddy Talamo and Joseph Provenzano, Gerry Chaisson and Pat Pecoraro, Andrew and Dianne Williams, Chef Andrea Apuzzo, Renata Zuppardo, Fausto and Roland DiPietro, Joel Randazzo Forjet, and Sean Cummings.

And thanks to the busy altar committee members at the Greater New Orleans Italian Cultural Society, the Center of Jesus the Lord, the Italian American Society of Jefferson and the Italian American Society of Jefferson Women's Auxiliary, Our Lady of Perpetual Help, St. Mary's Church, St. Benedict the Moor School, St. Mark Church, St. Joseph the Worker School, St. Cletus Church, St. Joseph Church in New Orleans, and St. Joseph Church in Gretna.

Thank you for the cookies.

This book is dedicated to the Eagan family, who lost Fritz on St. Joseph's Day, 2002. He is certainly watched over by the patron of fathers. And to my mother, who spent hundreds of hours with my new baby in her arms so I could do this work.

Joseph, the earthly father of Christ and husband of Mary, keeps under his beneficent watch fathers and families, workers and craftsmen, immigrants and travelers. The humble carpenter of Nazareth aids and protects expectant mothers and doubting souls. He is the champion of social justice, and the guardian of happy death. He holds the exalted position of patron of the universal church.

*Statue and votive candles at
Saint Joseph Church, New Orleans*

In the fifteenth century, Pope Sixtus IV officially acknowledged March 19 on the Roman calendar as the feast day of Saint Joseph.

He belongs to the working-class, and he bore the burdens of poverty for himself and the Holy Family, whose tender and vigilant head he was. To him was entrusted the Divine Child when Herod loosed his assassins against Him. In a life of faithful performance of everyday duties, he left an example for all those who must gain their bread by the toil of their hands. He won for himself the title of "The Just" serving thus as a living model of that Christian justice which should reign in social life.

—Pius XI, given in Rome at Saint Peter's on the feast of Saint Joseph, 1937

A luscious spread at the home of Frances Benetrix

Opposite page: *Saint Joseph's Table at the home of Angel Chevolleau*

Introduction

Every year around March 19, New Orleans awakes from a post-Mardi Gras daze to a faint scent of anise and red gravy.

Candles, flowers, and photographs of lost loved ones join statues of saints on three-tiered tables spread with a profusion of *pane, cuccidati, frittate,* and *pignolatti.*

This mysterious manifestation of an Old World devotion appears in parlors, churches, courtyards, and garages all around the city as small groups of the faithful prepare to thank Saint Joseph and ask for his protection.

A century ago, immigrants from Sicily, the largest and southernmost Italian island, brought with them *La Tavola di San Giuseppe,* a tradition of sacred spectacles honoring the earthly father of Jesus and husband of Mary. On his feast day, many of New Orleans' Italian American residents still offer food, wine, and flowers to the patron saint of Sicily, who is said to have delivered their ancestors from famine long ago.

Farmers or Fishermen, Exiles or Albanians: The Origin Legends

According to most sources, the Saint Joseph altar, also called Saint Joseph's Table, started in Sicily during the Middle Ages. As the legend goes, during a long drought and famine, Sicilians dying of starvation appealed to Christ's paternal provider for help.

> They pleaded to Saint Joseph, their patron, for relief from the terrible famine that gripped the island. At last the skies opened, sending down the life-giving water. The people rejoiced. Some time later, to show their gratitude, they prepared a table with a special assortment of foods they had harvested. After paying honor to Saint Joseph, they distributed the food to the less fortunate.
>
> —St. Joseph Guild, _Viva San Giuseppe: A Guide for Saint Joseph Altars_

Folklore tells that the fava bean, also known as the broad bean, was the only crop to survive the drought and saved many islanders from starvation. The hearty legume is thus known as the lucky bean and is a favorite talisman on every New Orleans altar.

Less-common variations of the origin story offer different theories about how the tradition began. Political exiles, fishermen, and feudal lords have been credited with building the first altar to Saint Joseph. It has even been suggested that the tradition began following the Sicilian Vespers, the island's bloody 1282 rebellion against French rule, when, theorists say, God caused a famine to punish the Sicilians for their own vicious acts against the French.

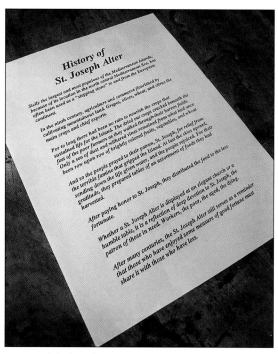

A copy of the legend given to visitors at Irene's Cuisine in the French Quarter

Lucky fava beans at Tony Marino's altar

Gumbo Ya-Ya, a collection of Louisiana folk tales originally published in 1945, includes a version of the legend in which dissidents were abandoned to the mercy of the sea:

> … in the Middle Ages a group of Italians were exiled from their country and set adrift on the sea in a small boat. In despair they prayed to Saint Joseph for guidance and protection, promising to honor him each year if their lives were spared. Cast upon the shore of an uninhabited island, they immediately erected an altar of branches and palmetto leaves and decorated it with wisteria, wild red lilies and other flowers.

Other sources suggest that the custom may simply have been started by generous Sicilian fishermen and farmers who invited hungry neighbors into their homes during times of scarcity to share what little they had.

Most scholars agree that a group of Albanian refugees called the Abreshe likely brought the Saint Joseph altar to Sicily.

David C. Estes, Ph.D., a folklorist at Loyola University in New Orleans, writes, ". . . the practice most probably arose in Albania, making the journey to Sicily in the late 15th century along with refugees from the Turkish invasion. The residents of historically Albanian communities on the island brought the custom to the New World in the second wave of its dispersion beginning in the 19th century."

Altar at Saint Joseph the Worker Church School, Marrero, organized by Chris Richard and Karen Haas

Opposite page: *Altar detail from the Brick Oven Café in Kenner*

Nancy Piatkowski, an archivist and researcher who studied altar traditions in Italian communities in New York State, offers an explanation as to why the tradition thrived in Sicily for centuries, serving a social, as well as a spiritual, function.

With Saint Joseph there is a hospitality and nurturing in the making and fulfilling [of] promises. In Sicily, in a society that is kin-oriented and closed to outsiders, the Table has provided a way for the women to open their homes to strangers in an accepted manner as well as fulfill the promise made to Saint Joseph. . . .

The hospitality of the Table stands counter to the intense individualism of the Sicilian society struggling against any outsider who attempts to take what is perceived as an undue share of their resources. Everyone basically says the same thing: "Saint Joseph provides." Thus taking the responsibility for the amount of food out of the realm of the secular and placing it in the realm of the sacred.

Across the Ocean: Sicily Arrives in New Orleans

Whether the first altar was made by Albanians or rebels, fishermen or farmers, tables throughout Sicily today fill with ornamental breads, flowers, and foods on Saint Joseph's Day as the devoted thank their protector and feed the poor, as they have for centuries.

Five thousand miles away, in the sitting rooms of shotgun houses and the transepts of gothic cathedrals, Sicily's New Orleans cousins also honor the patron of their ancestral homeland.

Wherever Sicilian immigrants settled, Saint Joseph came with them. Sicilian communities make altars in St. Louis, Houston, New York, Los Angeles, Chicago, and other cities, but New Orleans is the red, white, and green epicenter of Saint Joseph zeal in the New World.

The sheer number of Sicilian descendants living in the New Orleans area explains why. At over 200,000, it is the highest per capita population of Sicilians in anywhere in America.

A huge wave of Sicilian immigration hit New Orleans around the end of the nineteenth century. Fewer than 1,000 Italians lived in the city in 1860. Thirty years later, the count was 15,000, and by 1910, roughly forty percent of Louisiana's population came from Italy, the overwhelming majority from Sicily.

The French Quarter lost its French accent at the beginning of the twentieth century and started speaking Italian, with Sicilian immigrants making up ninety percent of the local population. People today remember Saint Joseph's Days of old, when palm fronds or japonica branches draped over every other door in the Vieux Carré, announcing an invitation to an altar inside. During World War II, the number of altars in the city hit its peak, as mothers and wives of soldiers petitioned for their safe return. So many altars beckoned in the French Quarter that it was impossible to visit them all. A tradition arose that you should visit nine altars in the neighborhood. At the ninth altar you made a wish and it would be granted.

Even before a great number of Italians settled in New Orleans, French Creoles celebrated Saint Joseph's Day as *mi-carême* (mid-Lent). Masked balls and weddings marked this break in the middle of the Lenten fast.

Opposite page: *Altar at the Center of Jesus the Lord, on Rampart Street, with a photograph remembering founding director, Fr. Emile Lafranz*

Above: *Petitions to Saint Joseph written on pieces of paper*

The Sicilian immigrants' religion was based on a close personal relationship with the local saints as patrons and friends rather than with God who was seen as a remote, unapproachable figure like the king. This feeling of a personal relationship with the Saints often led to the immigrants speaking to the statues in church as if they were alive rather than seeing them as symbolic representations of the Saints.
—Nancy Piatkowski

Saint Joseph in the Streets: Parades and Processions

Sicilian cooks don't simmer their *sarde* in crawfish boilers, and New Orleanians rarely hear the music of the *mandolino,* but some Saint Joseph's Day rituals in New Orleans and Sicily are very much the same. In addition to the altars themselves, both places have street processions to commemorate the day.

As night falls on Saint Joseph's Day in certain Sicilian villages, a statue of the saint rides above the crowd, carried on the shoulders of townsmen. A band follows, playing songs native to the region on trombones, tubas, accordions, and mandolins.

Like their counterparts in Sicily, 100 parishioners at Saint Joseph Church in Gretna (a suburb of New Orleans) carry candles and say the rosary, escorting a statue of Joseph from the church to its place on the altar in the parish gym on the eve of Saint Joseph's Day.

Irene DiPietro, a Sicilian native now living in New Orleans, describes a traditional Saint Joseph event in parts of Sicily as "like a mini-Mardi Gras." Flatbed trucks and horse-drawn carts laden with vegetables and fruit function like portable Saint Joseph's Tables and parade through villages, carrying food that is distributed to the poor.

In *Festivals of Western Europe,* published in 1958, Dorothy Gladys Spicer described the Feast of Saint Joseph in Sicilian villages the way it was celebrated a few generations ago:

A procession follows the banquet. The Holy Family, mounted on mules, is hailed by the villagers and given gifts of food and money as they ride through the streets. The celebration continues with singing, merrymaking, and rejoicing as the inhabitants dance about bonfires in honor of their beloved San Giuseppe.

Italian American groups around New Orleans take to the streets to honor Saint Joseph in a style akin to "dancing about bonfires." The largest Saint Joseph parade cavorts, Carnival style, through the French Quarter on the Saturday closest to March 19.

Members of the Italian American Saint Joseph Parade Marching Club continue a thirty-year-old tradition, strutting down Chartres Street in tuxedos, giving out lucky beans and silk flowers in exchange for kisses.

Daughters, granddaughters, and nieces of the all-male club participate as dance groups marching along the route, shaking their *posteriori* to blasting pop music. Other dark-eyed signorinas don formal dresses and ride perched on floats, including a fifteen-foot-tall altar float with fresh food, real fruit, and a four-foot figure of Saint Joseph on top.

Cultural Crossover: Non-Sicilians Embrace the Old World Saint

Above and opposite page: *Saint Joseph altars at African American Spiritual churches*

Right: *The Way of the Cross Spiritual Church*

In keeping with New Orleans' long and luxurious blending of cultures, other locals adopted this Sicilian saint. Many Irish Catholics pay homage to Saint Joseph and participate in the traditions, sometimes overlapping with the green-tinted revelry of Saint Patrick's Day. In one part of the city, Italian and Irish have combined their celebrations into a single parade.

"Everyone becomes Italian on St. Joseph's Day," says Lillian Moran, who calls in help from all the neighbors and parishioners to make the altar at Saint Mary's Church.

Non-Italians, and even non-Catholics, pitch in to help with their neighbors' altars, cooking massive amounts of pasta or donating cakes, lobsters, even egg rolls.

Since the 1930s, African American Spiritual congregations have joined in the Saint Joseph's Day tradition, building altars in their churches and filling them with Italian foods. Here, Saint Joseph, as the patron of social justice, is associated with Black Hawk, the powerful Sauk Indian saint at the center of the Spiritual cosmology.

Go to Joseph: Petition and Thanks

Ite ad Joseph—Go to Joseph; to Joseph of Egypt, the pharaoh told the needy to go for assistance to receive the grain that would save their lives. To the new Joseph, the just man to whom the Son of God Himself was subject as to a father, all Christians can go with confidence, and he will see to their spiritual and temporal needs with paternal goodness.
—Rosalie Marie Levy, *Heavenly Friends: A Saint for Each Day*

The act of making an altar and attending carefully to the surrounding ritual fulfills a promise made to the saint for an answered prayer, begs his intervention during personal crisis, asks him to watch over the souls of the deceased, or averts bad fortune. The covenant might involve one altar or an annual tradition that goes on for years.

There is passion behind the practice. A private altar represents a delicate exchange between the host and Saint Joseph that must be shared with the public in order to be

Left: *The Brick Oven Café. Owner Renata Zuppardo cooked all the food and decorated this shrine in memory of her brother, Silvano DiPietro, and husband, Mike Zuppardo. Also remembered on the altar is the niece of one of the restaurant employees.*

Right: *At the Lubranoaltar, prayers go to children in need.*

Opposite page: *Our Lady of Perpetual Help in Kenner remembers departed souls on the church altar.*

fulfilled. It speaks of the struggle for health and prosperity, the love of family, and the grief of death.

Some follow an old custom called *questua,* which involves begging for the ingredients or money to make the altar. Begging for the altar humbles the petitioner in the semblance of poverty and also recalls the starving ancestors in Sicily.

Individuals who cannot give their own altar keep promises by working on community or church altars.

It is believed that Joseph rewards each individual outpouring of effort and charity and will intercede to help in recovery from illness, the conception of a child, success in business, or the safe return of a soldier in times of war.

In Memory Of Deceased Members Of
St. Joseph Altar Society

Gus Trapani
1999

Mary Hightower
2000

Angie Pan
200

Franc
20

Gloria
20

In Memory Of
Florence W.
Thomas
St. Cletus St. Joseph Altar
March 19, 2003

"IN LOVING MEMORY OF OUR CHILDREN"

In Memory Of
Kathleen
Charamnal

In Memory Of
Tom & Gloria
Yash
St. Cletus St. Joseph
March 19, 2003

In Memory Of
Francis Edgar
Lutz
St. Joseph Altar
March 19, 2003

Francis Edgar Lutz

Previous page: *The altar at Saint Cletus Church in Gretna has a side table full of memorials.*
Above: *Joel Randazzo Forjet gives an annual altar at Randazzo's Heritage Hall in Chalmette in memory of her father.*
Opposite page: *At Angel Chevolleau's house, a corner shrine honors the family's servicemen.*

Generosity Marks This Day: A History of Charity

Generosity marks this day, as it did the character of Joseph himself. In many nations it's a day of sharing with the poor and needy. . . . In many Italian villages, especially in Sicily, everyone of any means contributes to a table spread in the public square as an offering for favors received from prayers to this kindly saint. . . .villagers representing Jesus, Mary, and Joseph are guests of honor at the feast, and other guests are the orphans, widows, or beggars.
— *The Catholic Encyclopedia, vol. 8*

The ultimate purpose of the feast is generosity. After viewings, blessings, and a ceremonial banquet for the "Holy Family," the profusion of symbolic cuisine is shared with the public and given to the poor.

"Widely diffused in Sicily, Saint Joseph's tables were primarily meant for directly feeding the poor as a form of communal, or public, charity," writes Luisa Del Giudice, director of the Italian Oral History Project. And today, like Italian American societies in New Orleans, groups in Sicily use altars to raise money for philanthropic reasons. "At public events," says Giudice, "food may be sold or auctioned, a donation may be requested for the meal or for viewing the table. In Sicily, significant funds can be raised by auctioning off Saint Joseph's beard [ornamental bread]. All proceeds and foods are then given to the poor."

A number of charities benefited from the Lubranos' altars.

Opposite page: The Italian American Society of Jefferson and its women's auxiliary give thousands of dollars, collected at their annual Saint Joseph's feast, to local and international aid organizations.

Saved, Cured, and Quenched: Joseph's Miracles

For more than half a century, local journalists have recorded stories touting the saint's miracles, tales of troubled souls who turned to Joseph—like Marie Cusimano, whose son was born on Saint Joseph's Day after doctors told her she could not conceive.

The most famous story is that of Charlie Licciardi, who survived a gunshot wound in 1980, thanks to the fava beans he carried in his pocket. Licciardi had been helping with the altar at Saint Joseph the Worker Church when he picked up some of the dried beans that had fallen off a table and absentmindedly put them in his shirt pocket. Later, as Licciardi returned to his business, a gunman robbed him, shot him, and left him for dead. He survived because one of the lucky beans deflected a bullet that would otherwise have hit his heart.

"While Saint Joseph's blessings are many, it seems he also can occasionally wreak havoc on an infidel or two," says New Orleans' illustrious food critic Gene Bourg, recalling a legend about a woman who promised a Saint Joseph altar. "Her husband refused her the money to buy the groceries and decorations. That night he retired early. Some minutes later the wife heard screams of pain coming from their bedroom. On entering the room she saw her husband's body covered with bruises. The next morning, she got the money for the altar."

Stories are also told of disasters happening to people who promised Saint Joseph an altar but did not keep their promises, like the man who decided to go fishing instead of helping with an altar and came back from the fishing trip missing one arm. One couple who criticized a neighbor's altar, much smaller and simpler than their own, were scolded by "a bearded man" and returned home to find their altar burned down.

But most of the stories relate Joseph's miraculous interventions and his blessings, large and small. Ethelyn Orso, in *The Saint Joseph Altar Traditions of South Louisiana*, recounts a story in which an old man placed a symbol of his request on an altar. The man, living at the Little Sisters of the Poor retirement home, wanted more beer served with his meals.

> He put a beer can with flowers in front of the statue of Saint Joseph and made his petition for more beer. A visiting priest at the home asked about the unusual flower container and was told of the old man's prayer. While traveling to another city the next day, the priest started chuckling to himself about the old man and the beer can. The man sitting beside him asked why he was laughing. After listening to the story, the man said that he owned a brewery, and that if the Little Sisters of the Poor needed more beer, they would get it. And they did.

The Trinity and the Cross: Essentials of the Altar

Whether intimate or gigantic, bright or subdued, sparse or spilling over, altars follow a basic form.

The traditional Saint Joseph altar is constructed in the shape of the Cross, with three levels honoring the Holy Trinity. One or more tables extend out from the altar and the whole structure is draped in white, anything from simple sheets to fine lace. A statue or picture of Joseph, often depicted holding the baby Jesus, stands at the center of the highest tier. Flowers flank the image of Joseph—especially lilies, the flower traditionally associated with him.

Typically, on the lower levels, statues and icons of the Virgin and other saints mingle with candles and photographs of deceased loved ones or people in need.

Previous page: Coordinator Angele Guient leads volunteers in decorating the altar at Saint Joseph Church in New Orleans. Donations collected go to the church's Feed Jesus program for the homeless. Constructed between 1869 and 1892, Saint Joseph Church on Tulane Avenue is the largest church in the South.

Opposite page: Saint Joseph Church in Gretna gives New Orleans' biggest altar.

Robert Zanca's charming altar in his front parlor on Tchoupitoulas Street

Petitions fill a glass bowl at Saint Cletus Church in Gretna.

Opposite page: Mudrica, *a topping of breadcrumbs symbolic of Saint Joseph's sawdust, on the altar of Frances Benetrix*

Some altars have a basket where visitors can place written petitions.

On every altar, the main attraction is food. Dozens of traditional dishes form a mosaic of devotion that might be strewn with oranges, berries, figs, squash, fennel stalks, grapes, garlic bulbs, olives, artichokes, stuffed peppers, and eggplants. Every kind of food flavors the celebration of the saint, with the exception of meat, forbidden in observance of Lent. Cheese is rarely seen on the altars. Instead of grated parmesan, a breadcrumb topping called *mudrica* is sprinkled on the pasta Milanese. (*Mudrica*, representing the sawdust of the carpenter, is pronounced and spelled many different ways around New Orleans. The word must have come from *mollica,* Italian for breadcrumb.)

A typical lamb cake on the altar of Madeline Console Bernard and Camille Console Meranta. A picture of their mother's first altar in 1946 has a special place on the table.

Every food on the altar has some traditional significance. The symbolism ranges from obvious to obscure.

Cakes covered in coconut take the shape of lambs, pastries form the pierced heart of the Mater Dolorosa, and whole fish symbolize the Miracle of Multiplication. Wine recalls the wedding feast at Cana. Sticky, sweet, pignolatti resemble the pine cones Jesus is said to have played with as a child.

Each visitor takes away a dry-roasted fava bean, the unassuming little nugget of good fortune. Carry a lucky bean in your pocket or purse, the legend goes, and you will never be without money. Fava beans come plain, painted like the Italian flag, and gilded.

Even the sour lemon, when blessed on the altar, is ascribed a sweet power. If you steal a lemon from an altar, you will meet the person you are destined to marry before the next Saint Joseph's Day. Stealing a lemon also works for luck in conceiving a baby. Or, if you find the *hidden* lemon on the altar and put it under your pillow, you will dream about your future spouse.

A pierced heart and other symbolic sweets at Andrea's Restaurant. Chef Andrea Apuzzo celebrates with a full month of Saint Joseph's Table flavors, including fava bean soup and Sicilian lobster.

Fish and wine symbolize Christ's miracles on the Fagot altar.

Pignolatti on the Fagot Table

Opposite page: *Diane and Andrew Williams' altar, with pasta Milanese, Saint Joseph's sandal, lucky beans, and pine cones (pignolatti).*

Piles of lemons with the power to help singles find a mate on the altar at Saint Mark's Church in Chalmette—Brenda Tromatore, chairperson

Bread That Can Calm a Storm

The essential symbolism of the altar is kneaded, cut, twisted, and baked golden brown. Large braided breads, *cudureddi,* shaped like wreaths, crosses, and Joseph's staff, take a place on every altar as the most important of the foods. The carpenter's tools—saws, hammers, and ladders—are replicated in puffy pane and covered with sesame seeds. Hard-boiled eggs are embedded into a sweet, round loaf called the *puppacolova,* representative of the rebirth of spring and the coming of Easter.

Similar breads can be found at religious festivals throughout the Mediterranean. Whether baked in the shape of a simple braid or made to resemble hearts, alligators, or crustaceans, the bread takes on its ancient role, exemplary of ordinary sustenance transformed into the sacred.

The baking of the bread may be viewed as a hallowed rite in itself. In some instances, the kitchen and utensils receive special cleaning and blessing. Silent prayers accompany the mixing of ingredients. A sign of the Cross sends the dough into the oven. And after the bread is blessed on the altar, not a crumb is thrown away.

Saint Joseph bread is believed to have a power especially important in New Orleans. Throwing a morsel into a storm with an entreaty to the saint is believed to have the power to calm the winds. A piece of Saint Joseph bread kept in the house insures that the family will never be without food.

Along with the soft, edible breads, many altars have another kind of baked art, symbolic pastries made from nonedible dough and used year after year.

Above: *Robert Zanca's cudureddi creations*

Opposite page: *The famous Glenda and Mike Lubrano altar in Metairie displays Mike's symbolic breads.*

48

Wreath, Cross, ladder, and staff made of bread on the altar at Miriam Murphy's home petition Saint Joseph to keep her Italian Irish family in good health.

Detail of the Lubrano altar

Fig cakes called *cuccidati* form intricate religious symbols.

Pastry and fig creations include chalices, hearts, crosses, fish, doves, lambs, and sandals. One common design replicates a monstrance, the highly ornamented container of the consecrated Host.

Opposite page: *Decorative breads and fig cakes on the altar at Saint Cletus Church in Gretna—Joy Hepburn, director*

A fig-cake Sacred Heart at the Chaisson & Pecoraro altar

The strangest of the fig-cake designs, Saint Lucy's eye pie, looks out from the Saint Cletus Church altar.

Opposite page: *Fig cakes crafted like fine lace on the altar given by the Greater New Orleans Italian Cultural Society at Holy Rosary Church on Esplanade Avenue*

Fill All the Spaces with Cookies

The baking of cookies starts weeks or even months in advance of Saint Joseph's Day—sesame cookies, anise cookies, dead man's bones, cocoons, iced fig cookies, and *biscotti* flavored with lemon, strawberry, and vanilla.

Thousands of cookies fill hundreds of plates, making sure there are no empty spaces on the altars of New Orleans. A list of instructions written by the altar committee at Our Lady of Perpetual Help reads, "Fill all the spaces with fruits, cookies, candles, bottles of wine."

Fig cookies waiting to be put on the altar at Saint Mary's Church in the Irish Channel.

Opposite page: *Cookies on Tony Marino's altar*

Heaven for cookie lovers on the Fagot altar

Opposite page: Fig cakes are a part of the artistic International House altar.

59

Pray for Us in Icing: Creative Cakes

Cakes of every shape and flavor come with messages, images, and icing roses. "Pray for us" is the refrain, written in sugar. Local bakeries create gorgeous hand-painted food-color saints. Some shops reproduce photos on sugar sheets to top sweet, frosted creations. Plastic pictures of Saint Joseph are also used to decorate the tops of *tortas*.

A redfish cake is a delicious favorite at Robert Zanca's altar.

Opposite page: *Frances Benetrix's altar displays homemade Bible cakes.*

Cakes may hold prayer cards, like these on the Zanca altar.

The Blessed Mother rendered on a cake at the Center of Jesus the Lord

Opposite page: *A Bible-shaped cake on the Saint Joseph's Table at Angel Chevolleau's home*

Cakes of prayer and remembering at the Saint Cletus Church altar

Honor Us with Your Presence: The Day Approaches

Local bakeries participate in almost every altar, donating breads, cakes, and traditional sweets. Some grocery stores offer a Saint Joseph altar discount on tons of flour, sugar, spaghetti, and other necessities.

For those not baking at home, Angelo Brocato's Ice Cream and Confectionary is the place to get authentic Italian cookies and sweets. Around Saint Joseph's Day, Brocato's adds pignolatti to the menu. They even make cuccidati crosses, staffs, hearts, and chalices for special orders.

As the day approaches, long hours go into preparing food and readying the house for a stream of visitors. Some still follow the old way of pushing all the furniture in the sitting room together against a wall and building the altar on top of it. The gift bags are filled with cookies, lucky beans, and prayer cards. Children are chosen to portray the Holy Family. A branch of greenery, usually a palm frond, is placed above the doorway.

Left: *A gift bag from Saint Mary's Church altar, containing blessed cookies and a lucky bean*

In the week leading up to March 19, the classified section of the New Orleans Times-Picayune *includes invitations to view Saint Joseph altars and join in the feast.*

Opposite page: *Angel Chevolleau's door, surrounded with palm fronds*

The Eve of Saint Joseph's Day: The Blessing

On the eve of Saint Joseph's Day, March 18, altars around the city open for viewing, and priests are busy blessing the abundant offerings of food and flowers.

Celebrant: O, glorious Saint Joseph, we stand before this Altar with joyful and grateful hearts. We lovingly present to you the labor of our hands and the dedication of our hearts that have fashioned this altar in your honor. We again place ourselves under your powerful protection. Help us follow your example of complete trust and faith in Divine Providence.

Open our minds and hearts to love and serve the poor, the suffering and those rejected or ignored by society. As a family, teach us to love and honor each member of our families with the love and reverence you had for Jesus and Mary. As a nation, inspire in us the will and the way to live in peace with all nations of the world, that in our day we can experience the fulfillment of Jesus' prayer—"Peace be to you." Grant this through Christ our Lord, who lives and reigns forever and ever. Amen.

V.: O Glorious Saint Joseph, through the love you bear to Jesus Christ and the glory of His name,

R.: Hear our prayers and obtain our petitions.

Celebrant: Lord Jesus, bless this altar, all this food, the candles and all those who visit it. We ask this in the name of the Father, and of the Son and of the Holy Spirit. Amen.

All: Remember, O most pure spouse of the Blessed Virgin Mary, my sweet protector, Saint Joseph, that no one ever had recourse to your protection or implored your aid without obtaining relief. Confiding therefore in your goodness, I come before you and humbly supplicate you. O, despise not my petitions, foster father of our Redeemer, but graciously receive them. Amen.

From the Novena to Saint Joseph:

Glorious Saint Joseph, spouse of the Immaculate Virgin, obtain for me a pure, humble, charitable mind, and perfect resignation to the divine Will. Be my guide, my father, and my model through life that I may merit to die as you did in the arms of Jesus and Mary.

Loving Saint Joseph, faithful follower of Jesus Christ, I raise my heart to you to implore your powerful intercession in obtaining from the Divine Heart of Jesus all the graces necessary for my spiritual and temporal welfare, particularly the grace of a happy death, and the special grace I now implore:

(Mention your request.)

Guardian of the Word Incarnate, I feel confident that your prayers in my behalf will be graciously heard before the throne of God. Amen.

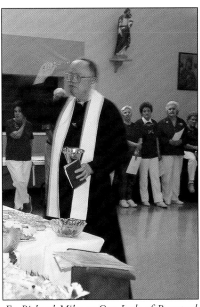

Fr. Richard Miles at Our Lady of Perpetual Help

Fr. John Capuci blesses the altar at the Center of Jesus the Lord.

Fr. Henry Engelbreght at the home of Dianne and Andrew Williams

Knock, Knock: The Ritual of the Saints

The *tupa-tupa,* Italian for *knock, knock,* reenacts the Holy Family's search for food and shelter. On Saint Joseph's Day, children portraying the Holy Family and angels are dressed in robes or fitted with wings. Joseph is sometimes played by an adult, and additional saints may join in the depiction. According to the custom, the Holy Family, also called the Saints, knocks at two doors and are refused:

"Who is there?"

"Jesus, Mary, and Joseph."

"What do you want?"

"We seek food and shelter."

"There is no room for you here."

At the third door the Saints are welcomed to take food and shelter in the home where the altar and a table await them.

"Welcome to this house. The table is set. The food is prepared. Come in and honor us with your presence."

The two refusals might happen at the doors of neighbors participating in the ceremony or the back door of the same house, or the Saints may even knock three times at the same door.

The Saints are seated at a table and served a taste of every item of the blessed food. At this "Feeding of the Saints," around midday on the nineteenth, the plates are constantly refilled to emulate the abundance Christ created of the few loaves and fishes.

After the Saints eat their fill, everyone else joins in the feast. In Sicily the meal begins with cheers of "Viva la tavola di San Giuseppe!" or "Viva San Giuseppe." In New Orleans they say, "May Saint Joseph always smile upon you."

Left: *Alyssa Marie Guillot portrays an angel in the* tupa-tupa *at the Center of Jesus the Lord. Gaige Rodriguez is Jesus, and Katy Cox plays the role of Mary.*

Right: *A table set and ready for the Saints at the Greater New Orleans Italian Cultural Society altar at Holy Rosary*

Sicily's Multicolored Bouquet: New Orleans' Variety of Altars

Each family or group adds its own tradition to the Saint Joseph's Day ritual and honors the patron saint of Sicily in a unique way. With this variegated collection of offerings rising on his day like a garden in bloom from faithful hearts all over New Orleans, surely Saint Joseph must, indeed, smile upon us.

Dianne and Andrew Williams
Dianne Williams asked Saint Joseph to intervene so that she might live just a few more months, long enough to see her son's upcoming wedding. Now cured of cancer, fifteen years later, Williams keeps her promise with the help of her family, giving an annual altar at her Uptown home.

Opposite page: *Fausto's Kitchen*
An intimate, candlelit sacred space is devoted to Saint Joseph at Fausto's Kitchen in Metairie, where pasta Milanese with stuffed artichoke is the special on March 19. Fausto DiPietro, born in Augusta, Sicily, honors Saint Joseph yearly with a vision of food, wine, palm branches, and lace.

Saint Benedict the Moor School
Second-grade teacher Christian Chiasson came up with an idea for a school project that became a tradition at Saint Benedict the Moor School in Gentilly. Chiasson and her mother, Annie, brought in Italian friends and relatives to help make a Saint Joseph altar in her classroom.

Opposite page: *Saint Alphonsus Art and Cultural Center*
The Redemptorist Fathers built Saint Alphonsus Church in the Irish Channel in 1855 to serve the surrounding Irish Catholic immigrant community. Now deconsecrated, the old church makes a dramatic setting for the huge edible offering to Saint Joseph.

The Alphonsus tradition started many years ago when Lillian and Sam Moran gave a small, home altar in petition to Saint Joseph the carpenter for aid in restoring their house. Over ten years, the Moran's table grew so big that they moved it to Saint Alphonsus, where it stayed for another five years. It has since moved across the street to Saint Mary's Church.

Marie Fagot

Marie Fagot and her family carry on a famous altar tradition that started in the French Quarter almost seventy-five years ago. One day in 1929, Teresa Foto returned home to find her house in flames, with her three children inside. Firemen tried to stop her, saying there was too much smoke, that there was nothing they could do. But Teresa pushed past the firemen to find her children, all the while crying to Saint Joseph that if he saved them she would build him an altar every year for the rest of her life.

Teresa carried her children out of the burning house and kept her promise to Saint Joseph.

Marie started helping Teresa with her altar in 1966 and eventually took over the tradition her friend started to thank Saint Joseph for saving her children. Marie's prayers for her own sick child motivated her work.

Today in their backyard in Lakeview, Marie's husband, Caryl, uses a 200-gallon crawfish pot to make gravy (a colloquialism for tomato sauce) to serve 500 people.

Caryl calls Marie the "whipper" of a group of ten ladies who do the rest of the cooking for the altar and the feast. Years ago they converted a garage into something of a Saint Joseph annex, with a large dining area and full kitchen.

The Italian American Society of Jefferson and the Italian American
Society of Jefferson Women's Auxiliary

Sal DiVincenti and Hilton Lirette cochaired the altar given by the
Italian American Society of Jefferson and the Italian American Society of
Jefferson Women's Auxiliary, a tradition that started twenty-six years ago
under the direction of Joseph DiStefano and Jack Montagino. This year,
125 gallons of gravy and 300 pounds of macaroni fed 4,000 people. But
that is not even their record—at the second annual altar, twenty-four
years ago, 6,500 people waited in lines around the block to sample the
array of Italian specialties.

Angel Chevolleau

Near the river in Chalmette, Angel Chevolleau turns her living room into an exquisite Saint Joseph spread.

Ten years ago, Chevolleau's mother, Candy Schlumbrecht, started the tradition with her daughter in petition to Saint Joseph to keep the children and grandchildren healthy and happy. Anyone may add a picture of a child in need to the altar at Chevolleau's house. Customarily, the tasty treats are off-limits until the altar is "broken" after the Feeding of the Saints, but children enjoy special privileges at Chevolleau's altar and may help themselves to anything they want at any time.

One year, Schlumbrecht's two-year-old granddaughter disappeared. They found her sitting in the middle of the big altar table, digging into several bowls of cookies.

Neighbors and friends tell of the miracles the two women perform in the kitchen—crawfish bisque, shrimp manicotti, eggplant parmesan, and gumbo, among other delights.

"I just dropped my traps and brought what come up," said a man in jeans, pointing out a plate of boiled crabs on the table at Chevolleau's house. "The ladies do all the hard work."

Opposite page: ***International House***

International House, a boutique hotel in New Orleans' business district, honors the city's Saint Joseph altar tradition by turning the lobby into a sacred space in the week leading up to March 19.

Sheer white tulle shrouds an antique wood statue invoking a vision of Saint Joseph's Day in Old New Orleans, when altars would have been draped in diaphanous cloth to protect the food from insects.

New Orleans designer Linda Sampson created this dream of palm leaves, amaryllis, pastries, cookies, beaded flowers, and Spanish moss. The unusual table features New York food stylist Zabel Meshejian's edible sculpture and her fruit-and-vegetable face modeled after the works of sixteenth-century Italian painter Giuseppe Arcimboldo.

Left: ***Chaisson & Pecoraro***

Gerry Chaisson and Pat Pecoraro have a long Saint Joseph altar tradition. Fourteen years ago, with her first altar, Chaisson asked Saint Joseph, patron of families, to help a family member overcome a drug problem. Since then, the family's altars have petitioned Saint Joseph to watch over a premature baby and heal a sister with cancer. They gave their fifteenth annual feast this year in a family member's home near Bayou St. John.

Pages 88-89: *The Center of Jesus the Lord*
The Center of Jesus the Lord, located in an old Carmelite convent in the French Quarter, recently started a Saint Joseph altar tradition. Coordinator Darlene Rodriguez led a group of volunteers who made the altar and fed 500 visitors.

Right: *Frances Benetrix*
"When you ask something for Joseph, make sure you want it," says Frances Benetrix, who has given more than ten altars in her Lakeview home. She remembers past Saint Joseph's Days when they served 750 people in three hours. Once they ran out of food and fried everything in the fridge, including pickles and celery.

"The Sicilians promised they would always, always make an altar for Saint Joseph because he saved them from starving," she says, "but it's a lot a work."

One of the Benetrix altars a few years back was dedicated to a girl with congenital heart disease. Everyone prayed for her, and against the odds, she survived. Frances broke the gender convention that year and let the little girl play Jesus in the tupa-tupa.

A part of the altar ritual for the Benetrix family is remembering departed souls, and the activity of cooking and decorating soothes the grief of the living.

Pages 92-93: *Frances Benetrix's living room on the eve of Saint Joseph's Day*

Talamo & Provenzano

After giving separate altars for many years, Buddy Talamo (right) and Joseph Provenzano (left) in Marrero teamed up to give a sizable altar and feast for 2,000 guests. Talamo and Provenzano dedicated the altar to their mothers and built a separate floral display for all mothers. They also made their altar distinctive by adding two adjoining scenes—a representation of a Sicilian farm and a trattoria *setting complete with a table, chairs, and* vino.

Previous page: *Irene's Cuisine*
Irene DiPietro gives one of the most famous and most sumptuous foodscapes Saint Joseph's Day
in New Orleans has to offer at her French Quarter restaurant.

The Rau Family
When Philip Rau was diagnosed with kidney cancer five years ago, his family and friends in Metairie baked and cooked and baked some more to ask for Saint Joseph's help. At the fifth annual altar dedicated to Philip's health, 1,000 guests ate baked fish, stuffed artichokes, fried cardoni, broccoli casserole, boiled shrimp, and lobster. The Raus went through fifty gallons of gravy and seventy-five pounds of pasta and gave away 35,000 cookies.

The Rau altar has its own little mysterious phenomenon—the Face in the Monstrance. Roland Fournier made a monstrance pastry that, when placed on the altar, appears to contain the image of a face.

Tony Marino

Tony Marino grew up with the Saint Joseph altar tradition in his Sicilian American family. So when it came time for him to take the bar exam, Marino remembered the saint his family had always turned to for help. After making his first altar and passing the bar seventeen years ago, he continued the custom in thanks to Saint Joseph.

In Marino's old French Quarter house, candles light the altar filled with fruit, cookies, stuffed eggplant, mirliton with shrimp, and baked cauliflower. Marino's mother, Mary, and brother, Kenneth, help him keep up the family tradition.

Pages 100-1: *Tony Marino's French Quarter parlor*

Previous page: *Bernard & Meranta*

Camilla deMarco Cascio came from Cefalu, Sicily, in 1892 and settled in the French Quarter, where her family opened a corner grocery. Today her granddaughters, Madeline Console Bernard and Camille Console Meranta, resurrect old family recipes and continue a third generation of the family's Saint Joseph altar tradition.

In Madeline's Kenner home, the sisters give the altars in memory of their mother, Rose Cascio Console.

Right: *Our Lady of Perpetual Help*

Deloris Plaia directed a large group of Saint Joseph devotees at Our Lady of Perpetual Help in Kenner in putting together a room-sized altar offered to Saint Joseph in petition for peace. She had no problem getting help. "People go all out for Saint Joseph," says Plaia. "He is a powerful saint."

Among the dozens of volunteers, Hazel Guidry stayed late to help lay out the spread of cakes, ornamental breads, fruits, and wine. Catherine Calamari and a crowd of other bakers went through 500 pounds of flour making cookies.

After Saint Joseph's Day, a big shipment of Saint Joseph cookies from Our Lady of Perpetual Help went to the soldiers in the Arabian Gulf.

Saint Joseph Church in Gretna

Parishioners at Saint Joseph Church in Gretna lend statues from among their family heirlooms to the largest altar in New Orleans. Coordinator Mary Trentacoste supervised a group of about 20 core workers who baked, decorated the immense altar, and hosted a feast for 3,000 guests.

Recipes

The following recipes from local Saint Joseph enthusiasts tell how to make some of the most popular traditional sweets and savories found on altars and feast tables.

In addition to the following dishes, lentil soup, an array of seafood, and omelets *(frittate)* round out the Saint Joseph's Day meal, along with a variety of fried or baked vegetables. In addition to the dry-roasted lucky beans, favas appear puréed, with garlic sauce, and in soups. Another old Saint Joseph's Day tradition is minestrone:

> *For this feast, a unique minestrone is made; people add any vegetarian ingredients that happen to be handy to the soup. [This is the origin of a Sicilian expression minestra di San Giuse, i.e., confusion or chaos.] — The Catholic Encyclopedia, vol. 8*

Cookies
Biscotti of Many Flavors
From Dianne Williams

5 lbs. flour	³/₄ lbs. margarine
3 cups sugar	2 cups milk
5 tbsp. baking powder	9 eggs
³/₄ lbs. shortening	1 oz. flavoring

Combine all ingredients and mix until smooth. To this basic recipe, add any flavoring you desire—vanilla, lemon, strawberry, pineapple, mint, almond, anise, etc. If anise oil is used, use only one teaspoon, not an ounce. A few drops of food coloring may be added to the dough to correspond with the flavoring—red for strawberry, yellow for lemon, green for mint or anise, etc.

Roll dough into small balls or make into rings or any shape desired. Bake at 375° for 12 to 15 minutes.

Chocolate Balls
From Betty Rau

9 eggs

2 tsp. vanilla

7 sticks margarine (use Imperial)

5 lbs. flour

8 cups sugar

2 cups cocoa

4 tsp. baking powder

2 tbsp. cinnamon

2 tbsp. allspice

1½ cups ground pecans

Beat eggs and vanilla in small bowl and set aside. Blend flour, sugar, cocoa, baking powder, cinnamon, allspice, and pecans. Mix by hand, then add margarine. Continue to knead until well blended, then add the mixture of eggs and vanilla. Roll into small balls. Bake at 350° for 15 to 20 minutes. They will crack a little on top.

When they are cool and *very dry*, roll lightly in powdered sugar or cover with an icing of confectioners' sugar, cocoa, margarine, and evaporated milk.

As with all the Italian cookies, they will stay fresh for several months as long as they are put away properly. Put in tin containers or galvanized garbage cans lined with waxed paper and sealed tightly.

Anise Cookies
From the Saint Alphonsus Altar

2 tsp. anise seed (or tsp. anise oil)   2 large eggs
8 tbsp. butter   2 cups sifted flour
1 cup sugar   1 tsp. baking powder

Crush anise seed. Mix with butter. Blend in sugar. Beat in eggs.

Combine dry ingredients and add gradually to butter-egg mixture and mix until well blended.

Shape into 1-inch balls. Place on greased cookie sheets two inches apart. Bake at 350° for 10 minutes until light brown. Makes 2 dozen.

[Green food coloring can be mixed into the batter or used in an icing of confectioners' sugar and milk. Make the icing a fairly light liquid and pour a little into a Ziploc bag. Put several cookies in the bag at a time and shake them until covered with icing.]

Biscotti Regina (Sesame-Seed Cookies)
From Pauline Canalito

2 cups shortening
2 cups sugar
8 eggs
2 tbsp. vanilla

8 cups all-purpose flour
6 tsp. baking powder
2 tsp. salt
1 lb. sesame seeds

Cream shortening and sugar. Add eggs one at a time. Add vanilla and blend.

Mix together dry ingredients and combine with the liquid mixture. Stir with wooden spoon until thoroughly blended.

Work dough into thin rolls about one foot long, as big around as your finger.

Roll dough in sesame seeds. Pat top of roll to make flat. Cut in sections about two inches long.

Place on ungreased cookie sheet. Bake at 350° for about 15 to 20 minutes until brown.

Amaretti (Macaroons)
From Mike Palao, _St. Joseph's Day in New Orleans_

1½ cups ground blanched almonds	½ tsp. salt
	2 cups sugar
4 egg whites	2 tsp. almond extract

Beat egg whites and salt until the mixture becomes frothy. Add sugar gradually, beating continually while adding the sugar. Beat until stiff peaks are formed. Fold in the ground almonds. Stir in the almond extract.

Cover baking pan with cookie sheet and drop teaspoons of the mixture about one inch apart on the cookie sheet. Bake at 350° for 15 minutes or until browned.

Makes about five dozen macaroons.

Pignolatti
From the St. Joseph Guild

5 cups all purpose flour	shortening for deep frying
9 eggs	1 cup sugar

Add beaten eggs to flour. Work with hands until a stiff, smooth dough is formed. Cut off small portions of dough and roll into pencil-like rolls. Cut into ¼-inch pieces and fry in shortening until golden brown. Drain on absorbent paper and let cool.

Melt one cup of sugar on low heat, stirring constantly so it does not burn. Cook until sugar is dissolved and reaches "string" stage. Place fried dough pieces into cooked sugar mixture. Pour onto working surface. With hands, form the sugar-coated pieces into pinecone shapes. Dip hands in cold water frequently to protect hands from heat.

Cannoli
From Emeril Lagasse

Cannoli shells:
1½ cups all-purpose flour
1 tbsp. sugar
⅛ tsp. salt
½ cup dry Marsala or other dry red wine

2 beaten egg whites
Vegetable oil, for frying
cannoli molds (tubes for shaping shells during frying)

Cannoli filling:
½ cup heavy cream
1 lb. ricotta
½ cup powdered sugar
2 tsp. nut-flavored liqueur

¼ cup finely chopped candied fruit
½ cup melted semi-sweet chocolate
¼ cup chopped pistachios

Into a bowl sift together the flour, sugar, and salt. With your fingers, work the wine gradually into the dry ingredients to form a stiff dough. Form into a ball, wrap in plastic, and let rest at room temperature for 1 hour.

On a lightly floured surface, roll out the dough to ⅛-inch thickness. With a cutter, cut out rounds 5 inches in diameter. In batches, as necessary, wrap each round onto a cannoli mold, sealing the edges with egg white.

In a deep sauté pan, heat the oil to 350° F.

Fry the cannoli in batches until just golden brown and crisp, about 2 minutes. Drain on paper towels, let cool, then gently slip the molds from the cannoli. (*Note:* Shells can be made 3 days in advance and kept at room temperature in an airtight container.)

In a mixing bowl whip the cream. Fold in the ricotta with a rubber spatula, working until creamy. Fold in the sugar, nut liqueur, and candied fruit.

Place 1 cannoli shell on a flat surface. Working from either end, fill the cannoli with the ricotta filling (using a pastry bag, if desired), pressing gently to ensure that the middle is filled. Dip both ends in the melted chocolate, then into the pistachios, and place on a waxed-paper-lined baking sheet. Repeat with the remaining cannoli and serve.

Makes 12 to 15 cannoli.

Sfinge di San Guiseppe (Cream Puffs)
From Allain Bush

The name *sfinge* is also used for "Italian donuts," a fried dough topped with powdered sugar, similar to beignets. *Sfinge* means *sphinx* in Italian.

Cream puffs:

1 cup water
$^1/_2$ cup sweet butter
1 tbsp. sugar
Grated rind of 1 lemon
Grated rind of 1 orange

$^1/_8$ tsp. salt
1 cup sifted all-purpose flour
4 large eggs, at room temperature
Optional: 1 tsp. Cognac or vanilla

Lightly grease a baking sheet and preheat oven to 400°.
Place the water, butter, sugar, lemon and orange rind, and salt in a large saucepan.

Bring the mixture to a boil and remove the pan from the heat as soon as the butter has melted. Add the flour all at once, stirring constantly and vigorously.

Return the pan to the heat, and stir constantly until the mixture forms a ball and comes away from the sides of the pan. Remove the pan from the heat and cool slightly.

Add the eggs, one at a time. Be sure that each egg is thoroughly blended into the mixture before adding the next. Stir until the dough is smooth and glossy. Cover and let stand for 15 to 20 minutes.

Drop the dough by heaping tablespoonfuls on a buttered cookie sheet, leaving 2 inches between the pieces. Bake for 20 to 25 minutes, until they are golden brown. Remove them from the oven and cool. If possible, wait until just before serving to fill, so they will remain crisp.

Fill with vanilla pudding, sweetened whipped cream flavored with vanilla or a liqueur, or a ricotta cheese filling, as follows.

Filling:

2 cups ricotta cheese
$1/2$ cup confectioners' sugar
$1/2$ tsp. vanilla

Optional:

$1/4$ tsp. ground cinnamon
$1/3$ cup grated milk chocolate (or chocolate mini-chips)
2 tbsp. finely chopped pistachios
Dash of crème de cacao

Thoroughly mix into the ricotta the sugar, vanilla, and any other of the optional ingredients. Make a horizontal slit in the middle of each cooled puff and insert the filling with a spoon or pastry tube.

Just before serving, sprinkle each filled puff with confectioners' sugar. Keep refrigerated if not served immediately.

Variation:

The cream puffs can be deep-fried instead of baked. For deep-frying, heat oil to 375° F. Drop the puff mixture 1 tablespoon at a time into the oil. Cook a few at a time, keeping the puffs separate. Fry until golden brown. Drain the puffs on paper towels. Serve them hot, sprinkled with confectioners' sugar.

Cuccidati (Italian Fig Cookies)
From Roy Liuzza

This recipe and the following, Saint Lucy's Eye Pie, can be used to make the fig-cake religious symbols seen on most altars.

Filling:

2 lbs. figs	1 or 2 cups honey
1 lb. raisins	2-3 tbsp. (each) allspice, cinnamon, and
1 lb. golden raisins	black pepper
1 lb. dates	Grated rind of a large orange
1 lb. nuts (mixed pecans, almonds, walnuts)	

Grind together in a meat grinder figs, raisins, and dates and place in a very large bowl. Chop nuts very fine and add to ground fig mixture. Add honey, spices, and orange rind.

Mix all this together until it is fairly homogeneous. Set it aside.

Pastry:

8 cups flour	2¹⁄₃ cup sugar
6 tsp. baking powder	5 eggs
1 tsp. salt	²⁄₃ cup milk
1 cup shortening	2 tsp. vanilla

Sift together flour, baking powder, and salt.

In another bowl, cream shortening and sugar.

In yet another bowl, mix eggs, milk, and vanilla.

Combine the egg mixture with the shortening and sugar and beat until smooth; combine this with the flour and mix until smooth.

Makes about 15 dozen.

Technique:

Note: The dough is easier to work if it's chilled for a while.

1. Gather a ball of dough about 3 inches in diameter; roll it flat, and trim into a 6 x 8 inch rectangle.

2. Take a 2-inch lump of filling and roll it in your hands like a cigar; lay it along the upper margin (short side) of the dough, about ¹⁄₂ inch from the edge. Take another and do the same for the lower margin.

3. Wash the filling off your hands and dust them with flour. (This is very important! If your hands are the least bit sticky or damp the dough will make an awful mess.)

4. Fold the dough around the filling on both ends to make a tube, then cut the dough

down the middle (shortways) so that you have two tubes of dough, about 6 inches long. Pinch the seam shut. Roll each tube out gently, pressing lightly and stretching until it is about 12 inches long.

Cut each tube into 6 pieces.

5. Repeat ad infinitum.

6. Bake at 350° for about 15 minutes, until the pastry is nicely browned. Turn cookies over and bake another 5 minutes.

Icing:

After the cookies have thoroughly cooled, they are ready to be iced.

2 cups confectioners' sugar	1 or 2 tsp. water (to make a smooth icing)
1 egg white	food coloring
½ tsp. lemon juice	Optional: nonpareils or chopped almonds

Mix all ingredients and divide into 3 or 4 separate small bowls; color each with food coloring. You can be tasteful or garish, as the occasion requires.

Dip the top of each cookie in icing (or spread a bit on with a knife); sprinkle with nonpareils (or dredge in a bowl of them). (I have heard of people who use white icing and chopped almond for a very tasteful effect, but my grandmother never did.)

Let the icing harden for a day before eating.

Saint Lucy's Eye Pie
From Patty Marino

Another version of St. Lucy's Eye Pie, rather than having eyes cut out of a top crust, has pastry eyes placed on the open fig cake (and no top crust). Opposite page: *At the Greater New Orleans Italian Cultural Society altar, fig cakes make a fancy dove, monstrance, staff, lamb, chalice, sandals, and other Catholic symbols.*

Saint Lucy was a Christian martyr who was blinded as punishment for her refusal to renounce her faith. A favorite fixture on Saint Joseph altars, Saint Lucy is the patron saint of the vision-impaired.

Step 1:
Enough dough to make 2 double-crust pies.

Line 2 bottom crusts with foil and fill with a layer of dried beans. Bake in preheated 400° oven for 8 to 12 minutes, just until crust begins to color. Do not overbake. Cool and remove foil and beans.

Roll out 2 top crusts to fit pie pans. Cut out "Saint Lucy's eyes" in each crust, leaving 2 empty holes. Cover and refrigerate until ready to bake.

Step 2:
2 pkgs. dried figs
1 cup raisins
1 cup dried plums (prunes)

Remove figs from package and remove any string. Place in a large metal steamer or colander over simmering water. Cover tightly and steam until figs are tender when pierced with a knife. Remove and cool figs. Cut into quarters and put aside.

Repeat this process with prunes and raisins. Cool and put aside.

Step 3:
2 large oranges
2 lemons
²/₃ cup pignoli nuts or blanched almonds

Cut whole oranges and lemons into 8 pieces, removing rind, seeds, pulp, and juice. Set aside.

In food processor with metal blade, pulse the pignoli nuts and almonds until coarsely chopped. Add oranges and lemons and pulse until finely chopped. Set aside.

In food processor with metal blade, pulse figs until coarsely chopped. Repeat process with prunes and raisins. Set aside.

Step 4:

Orange juice, if needed	2 tsp. ground cinnamon
1 cup honey	1 tsp. allspice
1 tsp. black pepper	¹/₄ cup red wine or port

In large bowl, combine honey, pepper, cinnamon, allspice, and wine.

Add all chopped fruits and nuts to honey mixture, mixing well with your hands until you have a thick paste that is not dry or stiff. Thin with a little orange juice if needed.

Fill pie shells with fruit-nut mixture. Top with remaining crusts.

Bake 30-40 minutes at 375°. Serve in thin slices.

Ciabatta Bread
From Irene DiPietro

Ciabatta means _slipper_ in Italian and refers to the shape of the small, flat loaf.

6 cups all-purpose flour	2 tsp. sugar
2 tbsp. dry yeast	²⁄₃ cup extra virgin olive oil
2½ cups lukewarm water	3 tsp. salt

Make a starter from flour, yeast, water, and half of the sugar, and let rise for 1 hour.

Mix in the remaining ingredients and let rise for 3 hours.

Knead the dough and let rise for another 3 hours, then shape into three 12-inch loaves, rounded at the end. Sprinkle with flour and let rise for a final 30 minutes.

Preheat oven to 475° and bake 25-30 minutes.

The recipe is time-consuming, but the long rising periods are what give the ciabatta a soft crumb and a thin, soft crust.

Variations:

Olives, onion, garlic, or dry tomatoes may be added to the dough.

Cudureddi, Saint Joseph's Bread
(Traditional Italian Bread)

4 pkgs. dry yeast
1 quart warm water
16 cups bread flour
1/2 cup sugar

2 tbsp. salt
1/2 cup shortening or olive oil
1 egg, beaten
sesame seeds

Dissolve yeast in one cup of warm water (100°-110°). In a large bowl, mix sifted flour, sugar, and salt. Using hands, mix together the dry ingredients, the shortening or oil, and the dissolved yeast.

Add more warm (not hot) water, until you can form a ball of dough. The dough should be a bit sticky. Knead until the dough is smooth and glossy, about 10 minutes. Place in an oiled bowl, turn it over once to oil the top of the dough, and cover with a damp cloth. Let rise until double in size, about 2 hours.

Press down the dough and divide. Braid and shape dough (described below*) and place on greased baking sheet. Let rise to double in size. Brush with beaten egg and sprinkle with sesame seeds. Bake at 400° for 30 to 40 minutes until golden brown.

*To make a simple braid, cut a medium-sized ball of dough into thirds. Shape each piece into a rope and braid together. Tuck under the ends.

Robert Zanca's altar includes breads formed into the alpha and omega symbols, for God, the beginning and end.

For a wreath, make a long piece of braided dough and bring the ends together to form a ring. With scissors or a sharp knife, make 1-inch cuts $1^1/_2$ inches apart around the outside of the ring.

To make a Saint Joseph's staff, form the braided dough into the shape of a cane. Flatten the dough slightly with your palm. Make cuts along both sides and on the top of the dough.

The same general idea can be used to create any shape.

Pasta Milanese
From Caryl Fagot

3 medium onions, chopped
3 tbsp. olive oil
2 (2 oz.) cans anchovies
1 (6 oz.) can tomato paste
1 (18oz.) can tomato purée
1 (15 oz.) can tomato sauce
$^1/_2$ cups water

salt to taste
pepper to taste
sugar to taste
4-5 bay leaves
1 small bunch fresh fennel
1 can macaroni seasoning with sardines

In heavy saucepan sauté onions in oil until translucent; add anchovies. Fry slowly. Add tomato paste, tomato puree, tomato sauce, water, salt, pepper, sugar, and bay leaves. Wash fennel and chop fine. Add to sauce. Simmer uncovered on moderate heat for one hour. Add undrained can of macaroni seasoning with sardines. Cover and continue cooking over moderate heat another hour until thick. Yields approximately 2 quarts.

Mudrica, Saint Joseph's Sawdust
The traditional topping for pasta Milanese is made using stale Saint Joseph's bread. Hard bread is grated into fine crumbs and browned in a skillet then mixed with a little sugar and sometimes a pinch of cinnamon.

Stuffed Artichokes
From Tony Marino

4 medium fresh artichokes	1 pint grated romano cheese
1 can of Italian-seasoned bread crumbs	1 whole garlic, peeled and minced
1 pint grated parmesan cheese	1 cup olive oil
	1 large lemon, sliced

Wash and trim leaves of artichoke. Mix breadcrumbs, cheese, and garlic in mixing boil. Carefully pull each leaf open and stuff with ingredients. Place artichokes in baking pan and pour olive oil over them, moistening the breadcrumb mixture. Pour water in baking pan to the lower level of artichokes. Place sliced lemons on top of artichokes.

Bake in 350° preheated oven for 1½ to 2 hours (depending on size of artichokes) covered, occasionally basting artichokes.

Let artichokes cool, place on serving platter, and garnish with fresh lemon and herbs.

Tip: You can serve the drippings from the baking pan in a small bowl for dipping or mix with angel-hair pasta.

Braised Fennel
From Tony Marino

2 large fennel bulbs
1½ sticks of butter
1 cup water

1 cup white wine
salt and pepper to taste

Remove tops of fennel leaves and save for garnish. Split lengthwise in 1-inch pieces.

Place 1 stick of butter in sauté pan over high flame. Place fennel in pan and brown both sides.

Remove the fennel pieces and set aside. Add the wine and water and stir with a metal spatula to loosen pan drippings and brown bits. Return the fennel pieces to the pan.

Salt and pepper to taste. Cover and reduce flame to simmer. Braise for approximately 20 minutes.

Remove fennel on baking platter.

Add ½ stick of butter to sauce in pan to thicken, using very low heat to avoid separation. Pour over fennel and serve. Garnish with fresh fennel leaves.

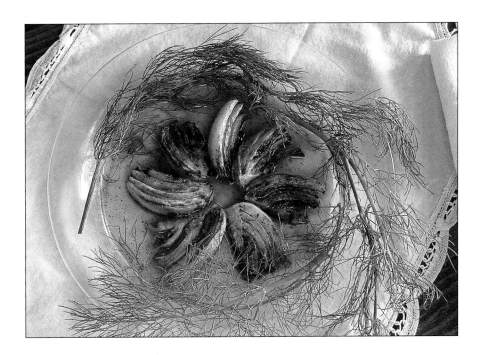

Baked Fish

From St. Joseph's Women's Club, Gretna

3 ripe tomatoes	dash of sugar
3 garlic cloves	1 (8 oz.) can tomato sauce
1 small onion	8 oz. water
1 carrot	1 tsp. oregano
1 celery stalk	$\frac{1}{2}$ tsp. rosemary leaves
1 tsp. parsley	2 tbsp. parmesan cheese
salt and pepper	1 3-5 lb. redfish

Chop tomatoes and put into pan with vegetables, all finely chopped. Add parsley, salt and pepper, and sugar. Add tomato sauce and 8 ounces of water. Simmer until the ingredients have cooked to a nice consistency. *[Clean and scale fish leaving the head on.]* Pour sauce over fish. Add lemon slices. Bake at 350° for 1$\frac{1}{2}$ hours or until tender.

Stuffed Pasta Shells "San Giuseppe"
From Patty Marino

Step 1:
2 boxes (1 lb. each) large pasta shells

Carefully boil pasta shells, a few at a time, just until tender when pierced with a knife. Do *not* overcook or they will not hold their shape for stuffing. Rinse in cold water and drain thoroughly.

Step 2:

2 boxes frozen chopped spinach,
  10-12 oz. each

4 tbsp. anisette or Pernod

1 tbsp. crushed fennel seeds

1 tbsp. lemon rind, grated fine

4-6 garlic cloves, peeled and mashed fine

1 tsp. black pepper

$\frac{1}{2}$ tsp. salt

$\frac{1}{4}$ tsp. freshly grated nutmeg

Thaw the spinach, then squeeze dry in a kitchen towel. In a large nonstick skillet, warm the spinach and all other ingredients.

Step 3:

1 (8 oz.) pkg. cream cheese

1 lb. chopped cheese (use provolone, fontina, asiago, chèvre, mozzarella, or a combination of any of these)

$\frac{1}{2}$ cup grated parmesan or romano cheese

$\frac{1}{2}$ tsp. black pepper

$\frac{1}{4}$ tsp. dried oregano

$\frac{1}{4}$ tsp. grated fresh nutmeg

Combine all cheeses and pepper, oregano, and nutmeg. Add to warm spinach mixture and stir until cheese is melting. (*Note:* You may leave as is, for more texture, but for ease in stuffing the shells, I recommend pulsing this mixture in a food processor or blender, then putting it in a pastry bag with no tip.)

Step 4:

4 quarts homemade meatless tomato sauce or any excellent store-bought brand

$\frac{1}{4}$ tsp. dried oregano

$\frac{1}{2}$ cup chopped fresh basil leaves

Preheat oven to 375°.

Combine basil and oregano with sauce, if desired. Pour sauce into 2 large disposable foil pans, making a layer about $\frac{1}{2}$-inch deep. Using pastry bag, stuff each pasta shell with enough filling to make a plump shape.

Set each stuffed shell into the sauce, filling pan one layer deep. You may top each shell with a dab of sauce and a pinch of parmesan or romano. Cover each pan with foil and bake about 30 to 40 minutes, until filling is hot and sauce is bubbling.

Serve each shell with a small amount of red sauce.

Mirliton with Shrimp
From Tony Marino

4 medium mirlitons

$1\frac{1}{2}$ sticks of butter

1 lb. medium, raw shrimp, peeled and deveined

$\frac{1}{4}$ cup diced red bell pepper

$\frac{1}{4}$ cup diced yellow bell pepper

$\frac{1}{4}$ cup diced green bell pepper

$\frac{1}{4}$ cup minced yellow onion

1 lemon

$\frac{1}{4}$ cup of chopped assorted fresh herbs (thyme, tarragon, chervil)

salt and pepper

Parboil mirlitons for approximately 10 to 12 minutes until tender. Do not overcook.

Cut mirlitons in half and remove seeds.

With a spoon, scoop out the vegetable, leaving the outer shell, and dice.

Melt $\frac{1}{2}$ stick of butter in saucepan or skillet.

Sauté shrimp. Add diced peppers and minced onions. Cook until tender but still crisp. Sauté for about 5 to 6 minutes. Add lemon. Toss in herbs.

Place mirliton shells on flat baking pan in 325° preheated oven for about 10 minutes, with small pats of butter.

Fill shells with mixture from sauté pan/skillet.

Place a pat of butter on each serving. Heat in oven for about 3 to 4 minutes to finish. Place on serving platter and garnish with fresh herbs and lemon.

Cioppino, Italian Fish Stew
From Irene DiPietro

Cioppino means *fish stew* in the Genoese dialect.

1/3 cup extra virgin olive oil
1 1/2 cup finely chopped fennel (save the leaves for garnish)
1 1/2 cup chopped leek
1 tbsp. minced garlic
1/2 tsp. dried oregano
1 tsp. dried thyme
1/3 cup fresh basil leaves, minced freshly ground white pepper
1/2 tsp. crushed red pepper flakes
1 1/2 cups dry white wine

4 cups shrimp stock
4 cups fish stock (from white fish)
32 oz. can crushed tomatoes in juice
1/2 lb. squid cut into 1-inch pieces
1 tbsp. saffron
1 1/2 dozen small cherrystone clams, cleaned
1 1/2 dozen mussels, cleaned
1 lb. large shrimp, deveined (21-25) kosher salt
2 1/2 lbs. fresh white fish (firm, such as redfish or drum), cut into 2-inch pieces

In a large brazier over medium heat, sauté the fennel, leek, garlic, dried herbs, minced basil leaves, white pepper, and crushed red pepper in olive oil for about 5 minutes.

Add white wine, stocks, tomatoes, and squid and bring to a boil over high heat, then reduce heat and cover. Simmer for 20 minutes, stirring occasionally.

Add the saffron. When the squid are tender, add the clams. Bring heat back to medium, then add mussels and shrimp. Reduce heat once again and simmer for 5 minutes.

Add salt to taste. Add fish pieces last. Turn off heat and let sit for about 20 minutes before serving. Garnish with fennel leaf.

From the Litany of Saint Joseph:

Joseph most just,

pray for us.

Joseph most chaste,

pray for us.

Joseph most prudent,

pray for us.

Joseph most valiant,

pray for us.

Joseph most obedient,

pray for us.

Joseph most faithful,

pray for us.

Mirror of patience, pray for us.

Lover of poverty, pray for us.

Model of workers, pray for us.

Strength of the home, pray for us.

Guardian of virgins, pray for us.

Safeguard of families, pray for us.

Comfort of the afflicted,

pray for us.

Hope of the sick,

pray for us.

Patron of the dying,

pray for us.

Terror of evil spirits,

pray for us.

Protector of holy Church,

pray for us.

Lamb of God, who takes away the sins of the world,

spare us, O Lord.

Lamb of God, who takes away the sins of the world,

graciously hear us, O Lord.

Lamb of God, who takes away the sins of the world,

have mercy on us.

He made him lord of His house,

and prince of all His possessions.

Let us pray:

O God, in Your marvelous providence You deigned to choose blessed Joseph to be the spouse of Your most holy Mother. We ask You to grant that we may deserve to have him for our intercessor in heaven, whom on earth we venerate as our protector.

Who lives and reigns world without end.

Bibliography

Berry, Jason. *The Spirit of Black Hawk.* Jackson: University Press of Mississippi, 1995.

Bourg, Gene. "Saint Joseph Altars." *Louisiana Cookin',* March-April 1999.

Bultman, Bethany Ewald. *New Orleans, Compass American Guide.* 4th ed. Oakland: Random House, 2000.

Chupa, Anna Maria. "St. Joseph's Day Altars." http://www.achupa@erc.msstate.edu (10 Nov. 2002).

Cole, Al, ed. *Viva San Giuseppe: A Guide for Saint Joseph Altars.* New Orleans: Saint Joseph Guild, 1985.

Del Giudice, Luisa. "Joseph Among the Angels: Saint Joseph's Tables and Feeding the Poor in Los Angeles." (2001) http://www.iohi.org/pages/joseph.htm (12 Dec. 2002).

Estes, David C. "Across Ethnic Boundaries: St. Joseph's Day in a New Orleans Afro-American Spiritual Church." *Mississippi Folklore Register* 21 (1987): 9-21.

_____. "St. Joseph's Day in New Orleans: Contemporary Urban Varieties of an Ethnic Festival." *Louisiana Folklore Miscellany* 6, no. 2 (1987): 35-43.

Maggiore, Raphaella, and Frances Centanni. "The Origin of the St. Joseph Altar. New Orleans Public Library, Louisiana Collection, n.d. Photocopy.

New Orleans Times-Picayune, 16 March 1997—18 March 2001.

Orso, Ethelyn. *The St. Joseph Altar Traditions of South Louisiana.* Lafayette: University of Southwestern Louisiana, 1990.

Palao, Mike. *St. Joseph's Day in New Orleans.* New Orleans: La Mar Management, 1979.

Plaia, Dolores, Sadie Pizzolato, and Mary Rita Pizzolato. "St. Joseph Altar." NewOrleans Public Library, Louisiana Collection, n.d. Photocopy.

"Saint Joseph." *The Catholic Encyclopedia,* vol. 8. New York: Robert Appleton Company, 1910. Online Edition 2000. http://www.newadvent.org/cathen (15 Nov. 2002).

Saxon, Lyle, Edward Dreyer, and Robert Tallant. *Gumbo Ya-Ya.* New York: Crown Publishers, Inc., Bonanza Books, 1945.

Spicer, Dorothy Gladys. *Festivals of Western Europe.* New York: H. W. Wilson Company, 1958.

"St. Joseph Altar Customs." New Orleans: St. Cletus Church, n.d. Photocopy.

St. Joseph's Women's Club Altar Cookbook. Gretna, LA: St. Joseph's Women's Club, n.d. Ware, Carolyn. "Ritual Spaces in Traditional Louisiana Communities: Italian, Nicaraguan, and Vietnamese Altars." *Louisiana Folklife Festival* (1992). http://www.crt.state.la.us/folklife/ creole_art_ritual_spaces.html (2 Dec. 2002).

Index

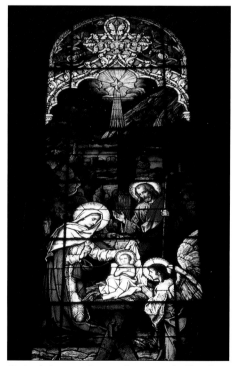

Stained-glass window at Saint Joseph Church in New Orleans